Jesus, I Feel Close to You

by Denise Stuckey

illustrated by Phyllis Saroff

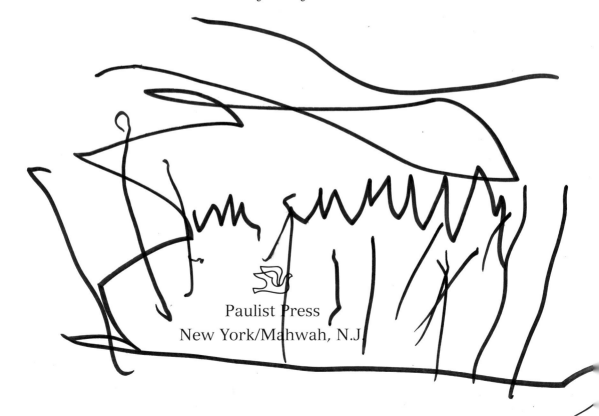

Paulist Press
New York/Mahwah, N.J.

Book and caseside design by Lynn Else

Caseside illustration by Phyllis Saroff

Text copyright © 2005 by Denise Stuckey
Illustrations copyright © 2005 by Phyllis Saroff

Library of Congress Cataloging-in-Publication Data

Stuckey, Denise
    Jesus, I feel close to you / by Denise Stuckey ; illustrated by Phyllis Saroff.
        p. cm.
    ISBN 0-8091-6718-2 (alk. paper)
    1. Jesus Christ—Juvenile literature. 2. Christian children—Prayer-books and devotions—English. I. Saroff, Phyllis V. II. Title.

BT302.S96 2005
242'.62—dc22

2004006596

Published by Paulist Press
997 Macarthur Boulevard
Mahwah, New Jersey 07430

www.paulistpress.com

Printed and bound in the United States of America

For you, Jesus. All for you.
—D.S.

For Jordan Culver
—P.S.

Jesus, I feel close to you
when I work with my daddy.

I think you must have worked with Joseph
in his carpenter's shop, too.

Jesus, I feel close to you
when I get lost
and I want someone to find me.

I remember how you got lost
when you were small like me
and your parents found you.

Jesus, I feel close to you
when I feel sick
and can't play outdoors.

I think about how you healed people
with just a touch of your hand.

Jesus, I feel close to you
when thunder booms and lightning cracks.

I remember how you calmed the sea
in that terrible storm.

Jesus, I feel close to you
when we have a picnic.

I think about how you made
a picnic for your friends
from loaves and fishes.

Jesus, I feel close to you
when I'm at the petting zoo.

I think about how you said
that you are the Good Shepherd
and I am your little lamb.

Jesus, I feel close to you
when I sit way up high in a tree.

I remember how Zacchaeus climbed a tree
to see you better—and you looked up
and found him there.

Jesus, I feel close to you
when I talk things over with my daddy.

I think about how you talked things over
with your Father, too.

Jesus, I feel close to you
when I have to carry my little brother.

I remember how you had to carry that big cross.
It was so heavy,
and you had to carry it such a long, long way.

Jesus, I feel close to you
when Grandma and I walk on the path
by the railroad tracks and find a spike.

I think about how soldiers drove
those big spikes into your hands and feet.
You hung there on the cross until you died.

Jesus, I feel close to you
when we explore a cave.
It's so dark and cold inside.

I remember how your friends cared for your body,
burying it in that cold, dark tomb.
They rolled a big rock over the opening.
Soldiers sealed the tomb shut and stood guard.

Jesus, I feel close to you
on Easter morning.

I think about how sad your friends were
when they came back to the tomb and found the stone
rolled away and your body missing.
But you were really alive!

Jesus, I feel close to you
when I watch the clouds.

I remember that you are up in heaven on your throne, watching over all that happens.

Yet, somehow, you live inside me, too.

One day I will see your face.

Jesus, I feel close to you
when I lie down to go to sleep.

I know you are right here with me.
You said you would never, ever leave me.
You love me, Jesus. And I love you.

Read About It!

The Holy Bible is a treasure book of wonderful stories. A list of every Bible story mentioned in these pages is included here with the hope that parent and child will enjoy finding them in the Word and reading these passages together.   —*The Author*

Jesus as a boy: Luke 2:40, 2:51–52; Mark 6:3; Matthew 13:55–56

Young Jesus is lost: Luke 2:41–52

Jesus the healer:
Matthew 8:2–3, 8:14–15; Mark 1:29–34a; Luke 4:38–40

Jesus calms a terrible storm: Matthew 8:23–27; Luke 8:22–25

Jesus makes a picnic:
Matthew 14:15–21; Mark 6:35–44; Luke 9:12–17; John 6:5–14

Jesus the Good Shepherd: Luke 15:3–7; John 10:11–16

Jesus finds a man in a tree: Luke 19:2–10

Jesus talks to his Father:
Matthew 26:36–44; Mark 14:32–36; Luke 22:39–44

Jesus carries the cross: John 19:16–17

Jesus hangs on the cross:
Matthew 27:33–54; Mark 15:22–39; Luke 23:33–48; John 19:16–37

Jesus' body is buried:
Matthew 27:57–66; Mark 15:42–47; Luke 23:50–56; John 19:38–42

Jesus is alive:
Matthew 28:1–15; Mark 16:1–14; Luke 23:55–56, 24:1–43;
John 20:1–30, 21:1–14

Jesus watches over me from heaven:
Mark 16:19–20; Luke 24:50–53; John 20:17

Jesus lives inside me: John 14:15–23, 15:4–7

One day I will see Jesus face-to-face: John 14:2–3, 17:24

Jesus will never, ever leave me: Matthew 28:17–20